HOPE THROUGH FAITH

HOPE THROUGH FAITH

JESUS CHRIST OF NAZARETH THE HEALER

By

JAMES FLETCHER

LYNX PUBLISHERS

DEDICATION

I dedicate this book to the good people at **The Turn,** formerly known as Return to Golf in North Olmsted, Ohio. And to the memory of Edward "Eddy" Bond and Mary Lou Lamb, who still inspire us today. I can't properly express the good work that these people are doing, so I will tell you more about that later and give insight into the glorious work that God is doing in North Olmsted, Ohio, through these wonderful people.

The annual Turn Christmas party Edward "Eddy" Bond is next to Rosemary in a wheelchair

PREFACE

Why write a book taking specific verses of the Bible and republishing them? I got the idea from Thomas Jefferson, our third president. Years ago, I was on social media, Facebook, and saw some people posting comments about the Founding Fathers' religious beliefs. One of the comments that caught my attention was that Jefferson was not a Christian and that he, in fact, wrote his own Bible, which implied that he didn't believe in the Christian Bible. This prompted me to buy a copy of the Jefferson Bible. What I found in reading his version is that history has mislabeled the document that Jefferson created. Jefferson named the document **The Life and Morals of Jesus of Nazareth**. In a letter that Jefferson wrote in 1803 to his friend Dr. Benjamin Rush, he expressed his idea to extract from the Bible only the words of Jesus. At first, Jefferson tried to induce others to do the work. Why would Jefferson want to do this? It's best explained in his own words: "We must reduce our volume to the simple Evangelists; select, even from them, the very words only of Jesus... There will be found remaining the most sublime and benevolent code of morals which has ever been offered to man." Jefferson eventually accomplished the work himself. He used a razor to cut just the words of Jesus from the Bible and pasted them into a book of blank pages. Jefferson spent many years working on this project, including while he was President; he did this not only with the English version of the Bible but also the Greek, French and Latin versions. Jefferson said, "I am a Christian, in the only sense he wished anyone to be; sincerely attached to his doctrines, in preference to all others; ascribing to himself every human excellence; and believing he never claimed any other."

I retired in January 2013. My daily routine while I was working was to get up at 5:00 am in the morning, be on the road by 5:30, and be at my desk around 6:00 am. After retiring, I found that sleeping in amounted to about 5 or 10 minutes after 5:00 am. So, I started to do something I've always wanted to do but never seemed to find the time: read the Bible every morning. I have done so every day since the day I retired. I found that almost every page of the New Testament had eyewitness accounts of healing the sick.

My wife Rosemary and I have been in a long battle fighting her multiple sclerosis, and reading those eyewitness accounts has kept me focused on the challenge with HOPE. So why not take those specific scriptures and put them together in one book to bring HOPE to others?

JAMES FLETCHER

THE SECOND LETTER OF PAUL TO THE CORINTHIANS

1:3-5

> *Blessed be the God and Father of our Lord Jesus Christ, the Father of mercies and God of all comfort, who comforts us in all our afflictions, so that we may be able to comfort those who are in any affliction, with the comfort with which we ourselves are comforted by God. For as we share abundantly in Christ's sufferings, so through Christ we share abundantly in comfort too.*

JOIN ME IN THIS PURSUIT FOR HOPE AND HEALING

MY FAMILY'S PERSONAL CHALLENGES WITH DISEASE AND DISABILITY

My wife Rosemary and I met in Jr. High School, she asked me to go to the Valentine's Day dance, the girls asked the guys back then for that dance. We have been together ever since and were married in 1972 after both of us graduated from college, Rosemary from Ohio State and I from Cleveland State. We were both able to find good jobs with two very good companies in Cleveland, Rosemary with Halle Brothers Co., and I with the Warner & Swasey Company. Halle's was founded in 1891, and Warner & Swasey in 1881.

Life was GOOD. Our leisure time was spent enjoying golf in the summer and skiing in the winter, and when we got vacation time, we would plan backpacking trips to national parks. We were always looking for new challenges, harder golf courses, more challenging ski resorts and hiking trails.

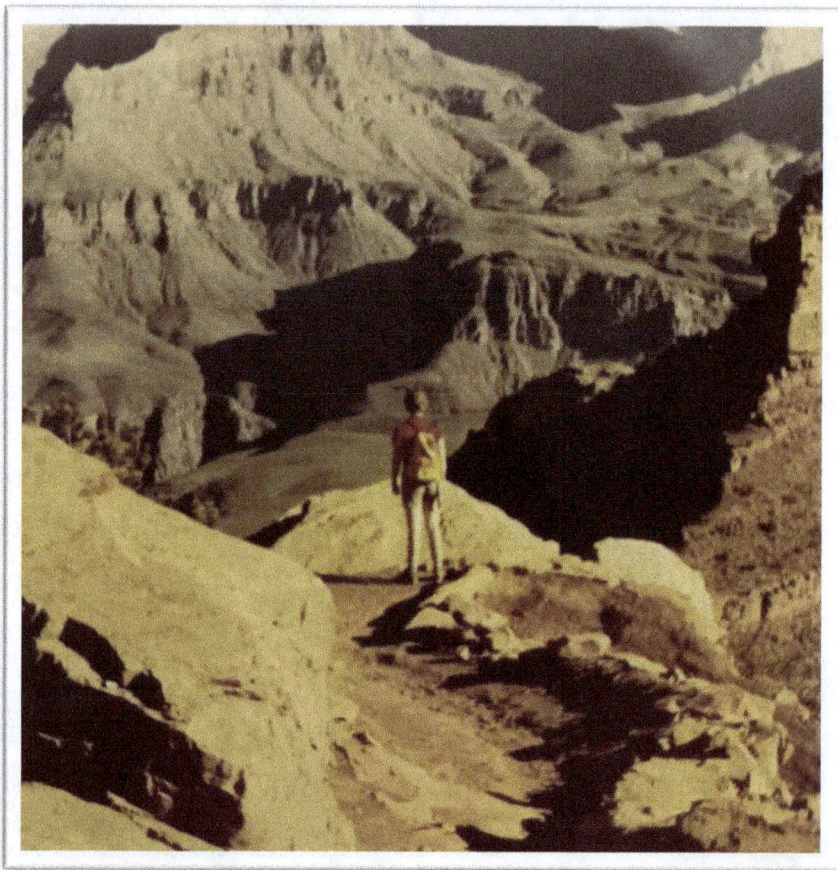

Rosemary hiking on the Kebab Trail to
Phanton Ranch in the Grand Canyon

One of our more memorable hiking trails was to the bottom of the Grand Canyon. We wanted to get overnight wilderness camping permits, but were denied because they were booked. So, we decided to do the hike in one day. We sought advice at a ranger station the day before the hike to talk to a park ranger to get some final guidance. The ranger's advice was that we should NOT try to hike to

2

Phantom Ranch at the bottom of the Canyon and back again in one day, the temperature was going to be around 100. The more he tried to discourage us, the more excited we got about doing it. It was a way bigger challenge than we had anticipated. We started the hike just at dawn on the Kebab Trail and hiked back out Bright Angel after having lunch at Phantom Ranch. It's an adventure both of us remember vividly even today.

MY BROTHER

I had an older brother, Charlie, who was 4 years older than I, and we became best friends over our lives. When I was 17 years old, he asked me if I would like to go to the Indianapolis 500-time trials with him. Of course, I said yes, what 17-year-old wouldn't want to go with their older brother in his '62 Corvette to the Indianapolis 500-time trials? We stayed at Y for a few dollars a night. We were so cool; it was Mario Andretti's rookie year.

My brother Charley and his 62 Corvette

When we were older, we would spend a lot of time together with our wives and other friends skiing in western New York and Colorado, going out to eat, golfing in the summer, sailing on my brother's boat, and going to the U.S. Grand Prix in Watkins Glen in the fall.

In the mid-1980s, this all changed when my brother became sick and was diagnosed with amyloidosis, a disease that had no cure and a life expectancy of only a few years. At the end of my brother's life, he was in the Cleveland Clinic, and I was working on the East Side. On my commute back home, I would stop and see him in the hospital every night. Quite often, my parents would also be there, and we would quietly sit and pray. My best friend, the big, strong high school track star athlete, now weighed less than 90 lbs. The day came, Wednesday, March 23rd, 1988, when I got the call at work from my father to tell me Charlie had passed away. He was 44 years old. It was a long, sad ride to the house we grew up in to console my parents.

My father passed away in 2003 at the age of 89, just two days before my parents' 65th anniversary. A few days before my father passed away, I was standing at the foot of his bed watching my mother hold his hand and say, "Nelson, everything is going to be ok, we are going to trust in God and Jesus Christ, and everything is going to be ok."

I was honored to give the eulogy at my father's funeral, and at the end of that eulogy, I said, "The hardest thing my father ever did in his life was sit in a room and watch my older brother Charlie die a horrible and painful death. That happened 15 years ago, and it's so easy for me to remember because my son Brian is here, and Brian was born one week to the day after my brother passed away. When those events happened, there was lots and lots of emotion, but for me, one of those emotions was anger... for how could God take my best friend from me in the middle of our lives. But through my father, I came to realize that God had actually blessed our family, for he had opened a window, and he gave us an incredible personal view of his love for all of us... for God had watched his only son die a horrible and painful death. We buried my brother on the Saturday before Palm Sunday 1988, and we all remember the story that's told every Palm Sunday. It is the story of a need to borrow a donkey and the owner of the donkey asking, 'Why do you need to borrow my donkey?' and a brief answer being given, 'Because the Lord has need of it.' So, I will offer those same words to you today as comfort, the Lord has need of my father. Please join me in a moment of silence so that each of us can remember a moment that we shared with my father on this earth. God bless you, all your wonderful family and friends." I think of my brother every day, and I am thankful he's still part of life.

The day after my father passed away, all our family attended the service at my parents' church on West Street in Berea, Ohio, to give my mom some support. My parents would have celebrated their 65th wedding anniversary in just 2 days. After the service, we all went back to my parents' home, the home we grew up in. As we sat in the living room, I remembered a Kodak slide photo of my father and me that was taken many years earlier. It was a picture of the two of us on a Boy Scout weeklong campout in Algonquin State Park on Lake Opeongo in Ontario, Canada. Dad was one of the adult chaperones. That was very special. My dad took vacation time just to spend time with me.

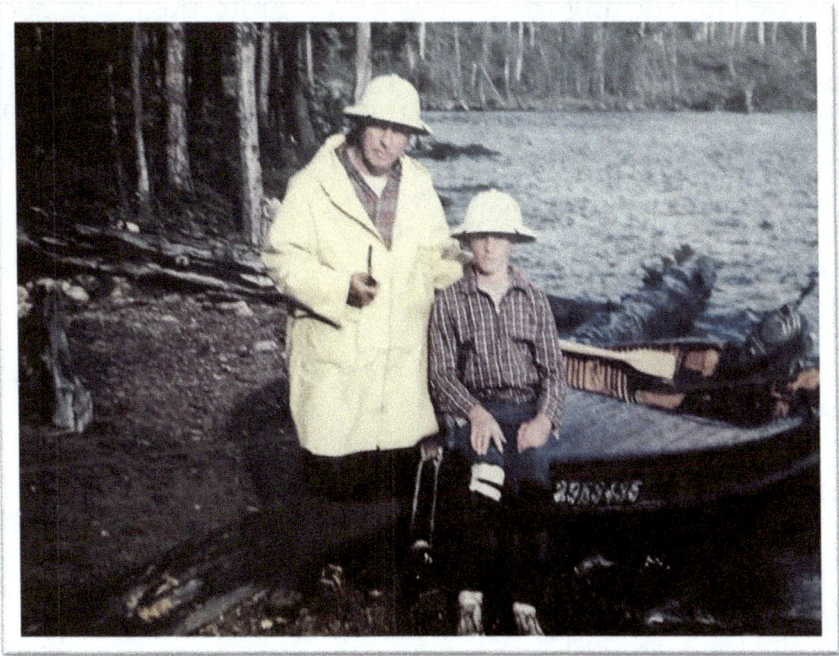

My dad and I at Boy Scout camp on Lake Opeongo,
Algonquin State Park, Ontario, Canada.

I went into the small den room at the back of the house, where I knew my dad kept all his photos in the closet of that room. I opened the door and stared at boxes of photos all the way to the ceiling. Thinking to myself, this is ridiculous, I'll never find this picture. I decided to give it a try and picked a box at random, and it was filled with trays of slides, and many of the identifications were worn off. So, I picked a tray at random and decided to just push out one slide and see what it was. To my great surprise and amazement, it was the exact picture I was looking for. I sat down in the big leather chair in the room, staring at the slide and starting to cry. I went back into the living room and told my family what had just happened, a small little miracle. I have that picture framed, and it's in a bookcase in our living room. Every time I look at It, I am reminded how blessed I have been.

OUR 40-YEAR CHALLENGE WITH MS

In 1984, my wife Rosemary had her first issue with multiple sclerosis; she was 35 years old. Out of nowhere, she seemed to have had a stroke. She lost her coordination and had slurred speech. She was hospitalized and they ran lots of tests, one being a CAT scan; MRIs were not available at that time. After about a week in the hospital, she was released and was completely back to normal. We didn't know it at the time, but that was the 1st challenge with relapsing remitting multiple sclerosis. Her medical diagnosis from the doctor was multiple sclerosis with a question mark.

Multiple sclerosis is a disease where the autoimmune system of one's body attacks the covering of their nervous system; the covering is called MYELIN. In layman's terms, it's like the wiring in your house with the rubber covering. When that rubber is damaged, you get a short, and that part of the system doesn't work. There are different forms of the disease, Lapsing Remitting, where you'll have temporary flare-ups and then times of recovery. The other form is Primary Progressive, where the person gradually gets worse over time. It depends on what part of the nervous system is damaged as to the loss of function that can accrue. It can range from inability to walk to blindness and a whole host of things in between.

It was almost 10 years later that MS came back from its remitting stage into our lives. Our lives had changed. By then, we were blessed with two children, Susan and Brian, and Rosemary had started her own retail store, The Pumpkin Patch Shop, an upscale children's store for grandmothers to spoil their grandchildren.

One weekend, we took the kids on a ski trip to our favorite resort in Western New York, Holiday Valley. The day was going to be spent on beginner and immediate trials with the kids. Rosemary was a very good skier; there weren't any of the black diamond runs that she couldn't ski with ease. But on this day, she was having all kinds of trouble falling, and after one or two runs, she said," I don't feel like skiing today," and she went down and stayed in the lodge for the rest of the day.

On the way home, we got into a little bit of an argument that something was wrong. She insisted she was fine, and I said we're going to make a doctor's appointment. That doctor's appointment ended up with her having an MRI, and with that new technology, the diagnosis was firm: you have multiple sclerosis. There was no question mark in the diagnosis now. The doctor told us there is no cure, but there were some medications that could help slow the progression down and minimize relapses.

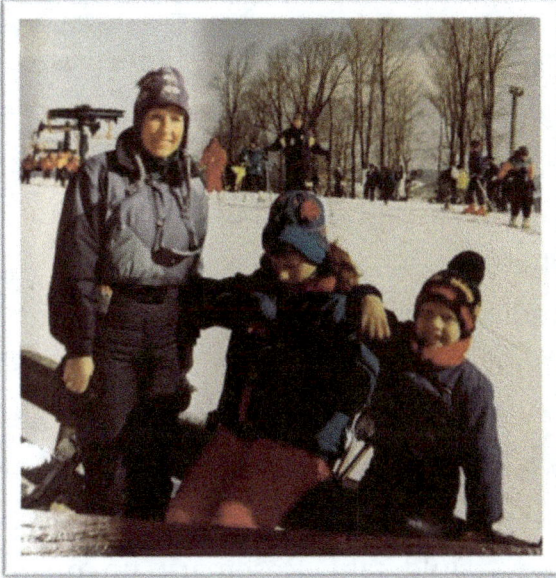

*The last day Rosemary skied. Holiday Valley NY
with our daughter Susan and son Brian.*

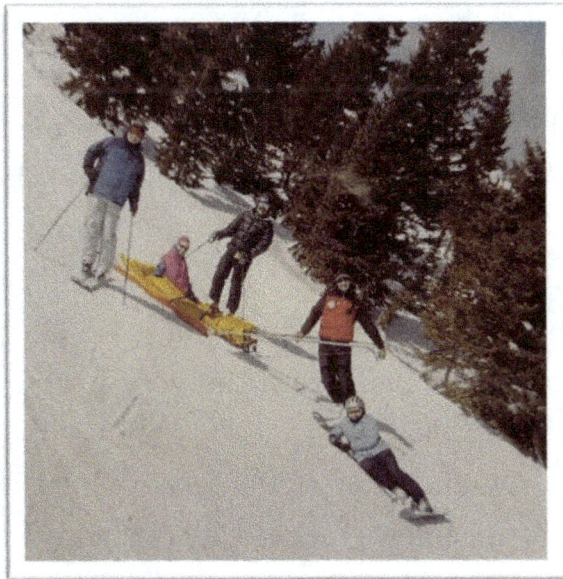

*Rosemary skiing with friends on the run Tranquility
at Wolf Creek with help from the ski patrol.*

We both knew a new challenge was now before us. She started the challenge with MS by taking Avonex, a once-a-week injectable medication that she had to self-inject. That day in New York with the kids was the last time Rosemary skied unassisted in her life.

In 2009, we were in Pagosa Springs, Colorado, visiting our dear friends whom we had met years before on a ski trip to Holiday Valley, NY. With a lot of help from the Wolf Creek ski patrol, we were all able to ski one more run together. Hearing Rosemary's plight, the head of the ski patrol suggested they could take Rosemary up on the mountain and bring her down on a sled, as it would be good training for them. So, they put Rosemary on a snowmobile, took her up to the chairlift, stopped the chairlift, put her in a chair, and she was on her way to the top of the mountain. They had another snowmobile waiting for her up top, and they gave her a brief tour of the views on top of the mountain. Then they moved her into the sled, and we all skied down together on the run called Tranquility. Another challenge was overcome, and we all got to ski together again with help from the very professional ski patrol at Wolf Creek.

On another vacation, we took our kids to one of our favorite cities, Quebec City, which is Canada's oldest city. On the way home, we were also going to explore Montreal. We stopped at a nice motel just outside of Montreal with nice facilities, a beautiful swimming pool and a hot tub. My son and I got into the hot tub after a swim. Rosemary wanted to join us, so we helped her into the hot tub from her wheelchair. BIG MISTAKE, within less than a minute, she became completely non-functional. We thought she was going to drown. Somehow, we were able to drag her out of the hot tub and back into her wheelchair. We took her back to our room and back into bed. She recovered in less than an hour. We learned a hard lesson that heat and MS don't mix.

The next time we met with her neurologist, we discussed that event, and the doctor told us that yes, the effects of heat can be severe for people with MS, and it's amazing how fast an MS patient recovers from that situation. With help from the MS Society, we did some research and found a vest that's designed to hold several ice packs. We keep that vest in our freezer, and if we're going to be out in the summer and warm weather, we bring it in a cooler. If she starts to have any reactions, we put that on her, and it helps very quickly. Another challenge was overcome with the right equipment.

In the late 1990s, Rosemary's relapses became more frequent and more severe. I remember one occasion when she was unable to do anything. We struggled to get her in the car to her doctor's appointment, and when we arrived, they put her on intravenous steroids. In a short period of time, 45 minutes or so, whatever time it took to empty the drip steroids bag, she had completely recovered.

After the confirmed MS diagnosis, Rosemary started to have frequent urinary tract infections. Many of these would put her in the hospital for five days with intravenous antibiotics, and then she would be released with five to seven days of oral antibiotics. After a few of these, we were referred to a urologist. The urologist did a simple test. He asked Rosemary to go to the ladies' room to relieve herself, and after which he did an examination. He used a catheter and emptied a large amount of urine that she was unable to do on her own. The doctor explained it was common for patients with multiple sclerosis to be unable to empty their bladder. A few days later, we were in the doctor's office with one of his nurses, and she took Rosemary to an examination room to train her on how to catheterize herself. After a fairly long period of time, she came out into the waiting room and said, "Mr. Fletcher, come with me, please; your wife is not going to be able to do this for herself." Rosemary had lost her fine motor skills in her hands due to MS. When we entered the room where Rosemary was, she was on the examination table with her legs up in stirrups. The very professional and kind nurse started to train me by telling me all the names of the private parts of the female anatomy. She demonstrated the procedure once. It was then my turn. After she made me do it twice, I was trained. I left that appointment thinking, Wow! This is going to be an interesting challenge. We have been catheterizing three times a day since then. Something like 30,000 times now, 29 years X 365 days a year X 3 times a day.

One happy surprise was after the first time we catheterized before going to bed. Rosemary slept through the night; her routine was to get up many times to go to the bathroom each night. I remember waking up thinking, Wow, she didn't wake me up. I feel rested. One small challenge overcome.

This new daily challenge has not stopped us from doing anything; we have traveled on a cruise to Alaska and a tour of Europe. You can imagine we've gotten ourselves into some very interesting situations. But everybody has been very gracious whenever I say I must go into the ladies' room to help my wife.

One occasion will give you some insight into what we deal with. We were in Colorado on our way out to see our friends in Pagosa Springs. We stopped at a nice restaurant for lunch, and it just happened to be the time we needed to catheterize. We went into the ladies' room in this old building, and the stall was so dark I couldn't see to perform my duty. My first thought was God help me. A second later, I realized, 'you dummy, you have a cell phone in your pocket with a light. Use it.' Needing both hands, I held my phone in my mouth for light. It was an awkward moment, but we got through it, one more challenge overcome. As I was pushing Rosemary in her wheelchair back to our table, I broke out laughing. Welcome to the crazy, challenging world of MS.

People who have to catheterize are in a bit of a catch too because their risk for urinary tract infections increases if they don't keep everything very sterile. We go through an awful lot of cotton balls and iodine. Unfortunately, Rosemary had several UTs at the end of 2020 and at the start of 2021. We had some real new challenges. She came down with a UTI on the day before the 2020 election and was in the hospital for 5 days. Part of that challenge was how she could vote. With some research on the Internet and a few phone calls, I met with the head of elections for Lorain County, and he walked me through all the procedures. Rosemary was able to vote.

Just a few weeks later, the day before Thanksgiving, came another UTI. All the food for Thanksgiving was ready in the refrigerator. My Thanksgiving dinner that year was some food out of the vending machine at the hospital, but we were together, the most important part of Thanksgiving. That stay in the hospital included some X-rays that showed that Rosemary had kidney stones, something we had dealt with too many times before. We made an appointment with her urologist, who said there was no urgency; the operation could be done in a few months.

Then came those 3 days in February of 2021, which we will remember for the rest of our lives. February 11th... another UTI and back in the hospital, February 12th, we got a call from our sister in law's sister that my brother's dear wife, Annie, had passed away from cancer. Then on

February 13th, we got a call from our nephew that Rosemary's brother had passed away from cancer. Remember, Valentine's Day is the anniversary of our first date back in junior high school. Meanwhile, this UTI was different. They didn't send us home like they had in the past. This time, after five days, Rosemary went home with the pick line in her arm, and they sent a nurse to the house to train me and how to administer intravenous antibiotics. Rosemary became so weak after all this that one morning, she couldn't even roll over in bed. With the help of prayer, we made it to March, when she was scheduled to have the kidney stone operation. All this was during the height of COVID. The kidney stone operation went well. But Rosemary had lost a lot of her ability to perform basic functions. We knew we had lots of physical therapy ahead. A new challenge lay before us.

It took two months before Rosemary could stand on her own using her walker for support and take two steps forward, one with each foot, then back two steps and sit back down. With HOPE, we have made progress. With lots of physical therapy at the Cleveland Clinic and lots of time at the Y and help from The Turn, she's 95% back to her baseline of 3 years ago of using a walker in the house and her wheelchair when we go out.

Rosemary's kidney operations have been a challenge. Over the years, I've lost count, but she has had all the different procedures: lithotripsy, ureteroscopy, and PCNL. After one operation, she was released and home, relaxing for only a few hours, and an infection set in. I had to rush her back to the hospital. It took five more days in the hospital to clear the infection. After the PCNL, they sent her home with a tube coming out of her back with a collection bag that we needed to empty. A week later, she went back to the doctor to remove the tube from her back. We successfully met every one of those challenges.

Rosemary had a fall a few years ago in our bedroom. When I found her on the floor unable to get up, I told her not to move and ask if she was hurt or had any pain, she said no, so we slowly got her to sit up. I asked again if she had any pain, and again, she said no. I slowly helped her into bed, where she rested. A few days later, I noticed she had a bad bruise on the right side of her bottom. I asked her again if she had any pain, and she said no. After a week or more, the bruise turned into an open wound. We had a regular doctor's appointment just a day later, and the doctor treated the wound and told us we needed to get a wound nurse scheduled to come to our house to train me on how to treat the wound long term. When the nurse arrived a few days later, she brought a wound kit that included cotton swabs, alcohol prep pads, petroleum jelly, Coloplast cream, and special bandages. I had to treat the wound every 2 to 3 days, and it took over two months to completely heal. Another challenge was overcome.

After the setback Rosemary had in February of 2021, part of Rosemary's treatments for a while included Botox injections in her right leg for spasticity; those treatments last for about 6 months. At her last doctor's appointment for Botox over a 2-year span, her doctor said no need to continue Botox. Rosemary has recovered. He concluded it was due to a combination of Botox and all the hard physical therapy Rosemary had done. Rosemary also has osteoporosis that was being treated with oral medication, but as the condition worsened, they changed the medication to Evenity injections once a month for a year. These treatments led to discovering a thyroid problem, and in December of 2023, she had a thyroid operation, where they removed 3 of her thyroid glands in her neck. The operation went very well. In just a month, she improved physically with better mental alertness. More challenges overcome.

In 2014, our son Brian came over to our house and told us about some lady on the internet who cured herself of MS with her diet. With a Google search, we found the lady's name, Terry Wahls, M.D. We discovered she had written a book, The Wahls Protocol, about her life-changing experience and within an hour, we had made the trip to Barnes & Noble and were starting to read the book. We read Dr. Wahls's book like we read our college textbooks with a highlighter, making notes in margins. To our surprise, Dr. Wahls, whose practice is located at the University of Iowa, was coming to our area to give a lecture about her research. Of course, we made our reservation to hear her speak. I can't get into details, but a few major points she lists in detail all the nutrients, vitamins, and the food sources for each. She also recommends a gluten and dairy-free diet. If you have an autoimmune disease or have a friend or family member who has the disease, I highly recommend that you get a copy of Dr. Walsh's book and read it. This protocol has helped us in our challenge with MS. Although Rosemary has not been cured, all her MRIs since she has been on that diet show no new lesions in her brain. That's scientific proof. I have other proof, which is that Rosemary wakes up on her own in the morning, comes into the living room in her wheelchair, fully dressed with her shoes on and tied, that's my simple daily real-life proof.

New challenges arrived in our lives in late 2024 when Rosemary had more urinary tract infections, which led to tests, X-rays, and an ultrasound that showed kidney stones again in both kidneys. So, they scheduled the first of the two operations for December 3, 2024. They operate on one kidney at a time. But that was changed because the oral antibiotics she was given didn't clear the infection. So, they did a different procedure on the 3rd and put in 2 stents to help drain the kidneys. They rescheduled the operation for December 16, 2024, and scheduled Rosemary to stay in the hospital for three more days for intravenous antibiotics before the operation. The Turn was having its annual Christmas party on the 13th of December, and Rosemary asked the doctor if she could go to the party first, then to the hospital at noon. The doctor agreed that it would be fine. We headed to the hospital after the party. When we arrived, they confirmed Rosemary was scheduled, but all the beds were taken. They advised us to go home, and they would call when a bed opened. We asked if it would still be that day. Their answer was that they were not sure. We got in touch with the doctor right away, and he talked to the hospital administration. He said if a bed wasn't available, we would have to reschedule the operation. So, we went home, prayed, and waited. Within an hour and 45 minutes, we got the call to go back to the hospital. As we were pulling into the drive of the hospital, the doctor called and said a bed is open. We said that we know we are in the drive now. He responded that he will see us in a few minutes. On December 16, the kidney operation went well, and Rosemary was sent home the next day. She still had a Foley and bag to help things along. A week later, she returned, and they removed the Foley. Kidney operation number one was over. Home for Christmas and New Year's.

The second kidney operation was scheduled for January 28th. Per test showed Rosemary still had a urinary tract infection, so she was again back in the hospital for 3 days of intravenous antibiotics. The operation on the 28th went well. Rosemary was sent home on the next day, still having the stents and a Foley catheter. The Foley and catheter were scheduled to be removed a week later February 5th. That short office visit went well, and now our lives were going back to normal.

Normal didn't last very long. The next morning, I was going to help Rosemary take a shower. While she had Foley, she was not able to shower for a week. Normal ended when she removed her top, getting ready for the shower, and I was looking at her back. It was all swollen and inflamed. She had a small cyst on her back for years, and we brought it to the attention of our primary care doctor at her last physical. His opinion at the time was probably ok, not to worry. The day Rosemary was released from the hospital, when she was getting dressed, her surgeon noticed the cyst, and we talked about it, and he too concluded it was probably ok.

Probably ok, turned into a very large, inflamed cyst. I knew we had to get medical help that day. My first thought was to get her to an emergency room right away. But thankfully, Rosemary had no pain and no knowledge that she even had a problem. I took a picture to show her what we were dealing with. So, we decided to give her a shower, have breakfast and call our primary care doctor. I made the call at 9:00 am and they said they had an opening at 10:00. I immediately responded that we would take it. With today's modern technology, I sent them the picture, so they knew what we were dealing with before we arrived. After seeing the wound, the nurse quickly referred us to a surgeon, who confirmed that surgery was needed. We discussed two options for the surgery, in the office using local anesthesia or do it in the operating room using general anesthesia. We asked what he thought would be best for Rosemary. He recommended the operating room. After learning Rosemary had last eaten at 9:00 a.m., he postponed the operation until 3:30 p.m. They needed to wait 6 hours before general anesthesia. The surgery took about 30 minutes, and it went well. In the recovery room, they gave me detailed instructions on how I would have to change bandages on the wound daily. On the way home, we stopped at the pharmacy to pick up some pain medication.

The next day, when I went to change the bandage, I was not prepared to see what we were dealing with. After removing the large bandage, I was looking at a 4-inch-long by 1 ½ inch wide wound with no skin. After my initial shock, I asked God to help me focus and do what the doctor and nurse had told me. Thankfully, Rosemary had no pain and didn't need the pain medication. We had a follow-up with the doctor a week later, and he showed me a small amount of new skin healing and how to dress the wound going forward. He was pleased with what he saw and said that he would see us in 2 weeks. He also said it will take months to completely heal. One more challenge we had to work our way through with God's help.

THE "TURN" A COMMUNITY OF HOPE

My wife is a member of The Turn in North Olmsted, the program I mentioned in the dedication. This group of disabled people are some of the most upbeat, Hopeful people I have ever met in my life.

Rosemary with Mary Lou Lamb a past member of The Turn

In 2014, I was finishing a round of golf at one of our public courses. While I was walking back to the clubhouse, I noticed a man in a single-rider golf cart. He was clearly disabled, waiting to tee off on number one. I approached him and politely asked if he wouldn't mind talking to me. He was very gracious and said, "Not at all." I explained to him the situation with my wife, and he replied, "Oh, there is a program over at North Olmsted called Return to Golf for Disabled people."

I thanked him and walked back up towards the clubhouse, but still in clear view of the first tee. I wanted to watch him hit his tee ball. To my delight, he hit a very nice drive in the fairway. On the way home, I called Rosemary and told her what I saw, and I told her you're going to play golf again, and she said I was crazy. The next day, we went over to the North Olmsted golf course to check things out, and after we got an ok from Rosemary's doctor, a few days later, she was getting her first lesson on how to use a single rider golf cart. Rosemary had not played golf since that day in N.Y. when she fell skiing. We played our first round of golf together again after many years on her 65th birthday. It was one of the best, MOST ENJOYABLE, rounds I have ever played. Another challenge was overcome with help from the wonderful people at THE TURN and special equipment. This year, we celebrate our 11th anniversary with THE TURN.

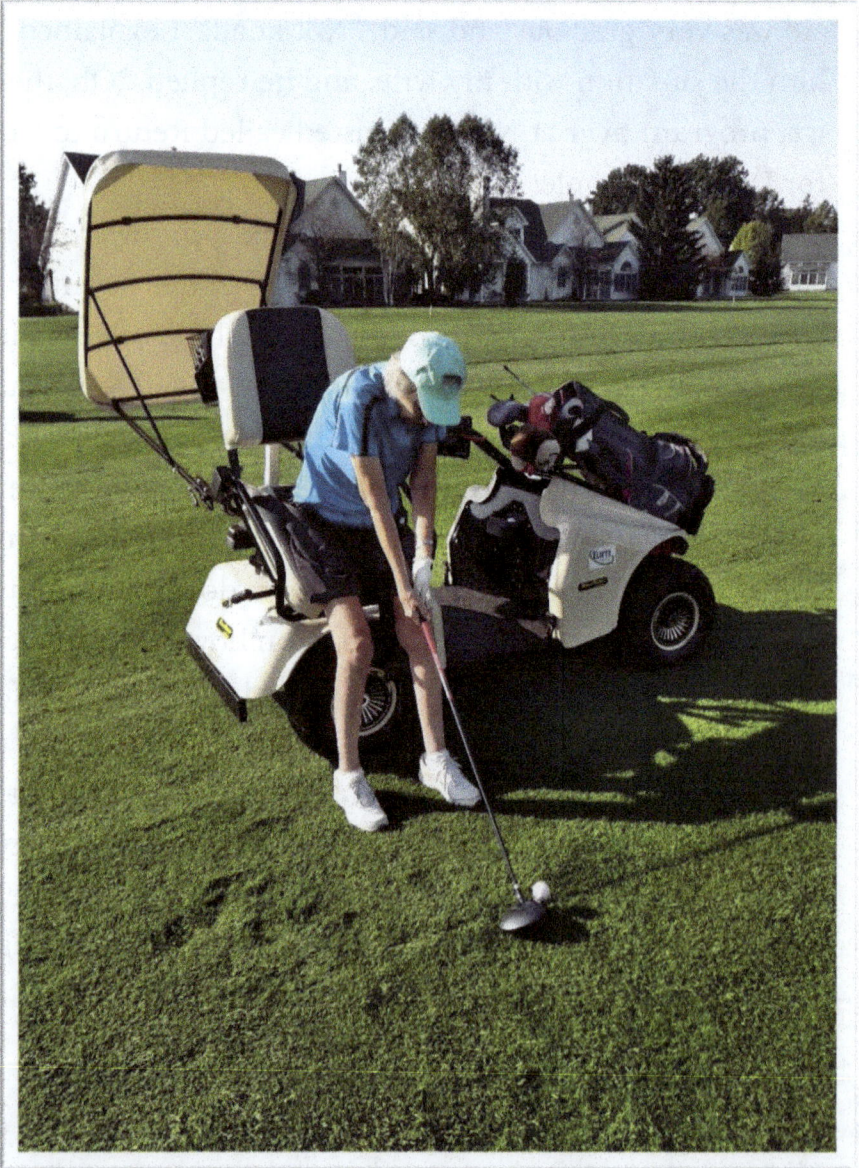

Rosemary playing golf with the help of a Solo-Rider golf cart.

FROM THE TURN'S WEBSITE

The TURN is dedicated to ENHANCING THE HEALTH AND WELL-BEING OF PEOPLE WITH PHYSICAL DISABILITIES.

WHY WE DO WHAT WE DO: It is said that the most important shot in the game of golf is the next one. The same applies to someone whose life has been impacted by a physical disability. Whether recovering from a stroke, amputation, or traumatic brain injury, what a person with physical disability does next following their rehabilitation can make all the difference in the "next chapter" of quality of life, getting individuals back on course to thrive both physically and emotionally.

WHO WE SERVE: Participants – from juniors to adults and veterans- represent a broad range of physical disabilities, including stroke survivors and amputees, and those with traumatic brain injuries, visual impairment, multiple sclerosis, cerebral palsy and Parkinson's disease.

WHAT WE DO: We offer year-round individual and group programs, providing non-clinical adaptive fitness and recreation opportunities to improve balance, coordination, muscle strength, and, most importantly, build self-esteem

WHO WE ARE: A team of dedicated PGA golf professionals, certified fitness instructors, support staff from the rehabilitation and sports therapy departments of

Greater Cleveland's leading hospital systems, passionate volunteers, and loyal donors. Our 15-acre campus, located at the North Olmsted Golf Club, offers one-of-a-kind barrier-free access to an adaptive fitness center, indoor golf learning center, and nine-hole accessible golf course, as well as the region's largest fleet of adaptive golf vehicles.

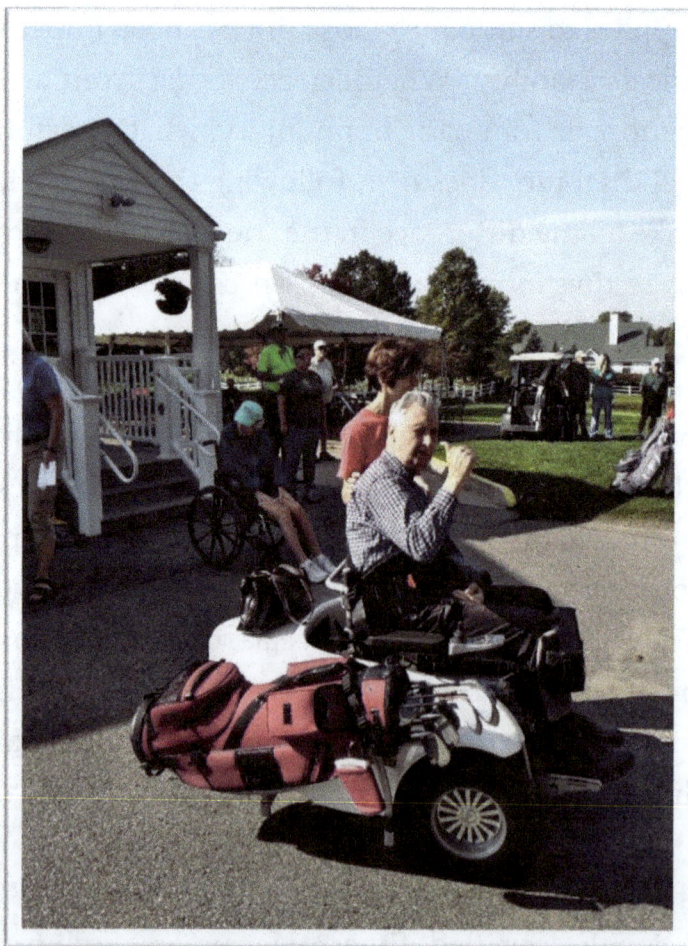

Dan Papcun, after his stroke going out for a round of golf with help from the people at The Turn

HOW WE ARE DIFFERENT: The Turn is more than a place or a program; it is a purpose and a community for people living with physical disabilities to enhance their physical and emotional needs.

The Pro vs. The Legend

September 26, 2023

On Sunday, September 24, a match was held at North Olmsted Golf Club between 'The Pro' Erin Craig, PGA head golf professional for The Turn, and 'The Legend', longtime Turn member Herb Werner.

The two were to play in a head-to-head match with one unique provision: Erin had to use the same type of adaptive vehicle as Herb.

In the end, Herb outlasted Erin 42-45 for the victory, as scores of spectators looked on.

The following day, Herb sent the following email to Erin.

TO: Erin Craig
FROM: Herb Werner

Dear PRO,
Sunday, September 24, 2023, will be a special memory for me. The opportunity to have a challenging golf game

with both of us using adaptive equipment was an outstanding experience. At no time during the event did I give a single thought to my physical limitations. Instead, I recognized what a great opportunity I was being given to participate in a challenging, positive, and "normal" event. I appreciate you taking the time to learn some of the challenges that members of the disability community experience on their continuing journey through life. This is another example of why I describe THE TURN as the Demonstration Laboratory for assisting people in the quest for a productive and rewarding quality of life. Please know that you are truly making a difference in countless lives. I am proud to refer to you as my PRO!

My wife and I were not able to attend the match between Erin and Herb. But we were privileged to witness a similar match between Erin and a junior member, a high school boy who is blind. Erin, in that match, had to play blindfolded. I've been fortunate enough to watch the pros play at Firestone, but the match between Erin and the high school boy was the best I've ever seen.

A few years ago, my sister's brother-in-law, Danny Papcun, had a stroke. Soon after it happened, we went to visit him in the hospital, and I had a conversation to offer support for his wife, Sherry. I told her about what their future would hold for them, and that Danny would play golf with us. Well, after a long recovery with lots of physical therapy, Danny was able to join The Turn. It's been wonderful to see him continue to make progress with help from the people at The Turn, moving on from a Paramobile cart to a SoloRider golf cart. The last two years, our family has been able to play in the annual Turn golf scramble and luncheon, where family and friends get to join in the fun and play a round of golf together, and celebrate the blessings of family and friends. Prayers do get answered.

THE EYEWITNESS ACCOUNTS OF HEALING BY JESUS CHRIST OF NAZARETH

It is my sincere wish that the following words bring hope to those dealing with illness and disease, both those who are directly affected and the caregivers who support them.

Matthew

4:23-25

And he went about all Galilee, teaching in their synagogues and preaching the gospel of the kingdom and healing every disease and every infirmity among the people. So, his fame spread throughout all Syria, and they brought him all the sick, those affiliated with various diseases, and pains, demoniacs, and paralytics, and he healed them. And great crowds followed him from Galilee and the Decapolis and Jerusalem and Judea and from beyond the Jordan.

8:1-4

When he came down from the mountain, great crowds followed him; and behold, a leper came to him and knelt before him, saying, "Lord, if you will, you can make me clean." And immediately his leprosy was cleansed. And Jesus said to him, "See that you say nothing to anyone; but go, show yourself to the priest, and offer the gift that Moses commanded, for a proof of the people."

8:5-13

As he entered Capernaum, a centurion came forward to him, beseeching him and saying, "Lord, my servant is lying paralyzed at home, in terrible distress." And he said to him, "I will come and heal him." But the centurion answered him, "Lord, I am not worthy to have come under my roof; but only say the word, and my servant will be healed. For I am a man under authority, with soldiers under me; and I say to one, 'Go,' and he goes, and to another, 'Come,' and he comes, and to my slave, 'Do this,' and he does it." When Jesus heard him, he marveled and said to those who followed him, "Truly, I say to you, not even in Israel have I found such faith. I tell you, many will come from east and west and sit at table with Abraham, Isaac, and Jacob in the kingdom of heaven, while the sons of the kingdom will be thrown into the outer darkness; there men will weep and gnash their teeth." And to the centurion, Jesus said, "Go; be it done for you as you have believed." And the servant was healed at that very moment.

8:14-17

And when Jesus entered Peter's house, he saw his mother-in-law lying sick with a fever; he touched her hand, and the fever left her, and she rose and served him. That evening, they brought to him many who were possessed with demons; and he cast out the spirits with a word, and healed all who were sick. This was to fulfil what was spoken by the prophet Isaiah, "He took our infirmities and bore our diseases."

9:2-7

And behold, they brought to him a paralytic, lying on his bed; and when Jesus saw their faith, he said to the paralytic, "Take heart, my son; your sins are forgiven." And behold, some of the scribes said to themselves, "This man is blaspheming." But Jesus, knowing their thoughts, said, "Why do you think evil in your hearts? For which is easier, to say, 'Your sins are forgiven,' or to say, 'Rise and walk'? But that you may know that the Son of man has authority on earth to forgive sins" – he then said to the paralytic - "Rise, take up your bed and go home." And he rose and went home.

9:18-26

While he was thus speaking to them, a ruler came in and knelt before him, saying, "My daughter has just died; but come and lay your hands on her, and she will live." And Jesus rose and followed him, with his disciples. And behold, a woman who had suffered from a hemorrhage for twelve years came up behind him, touched the fringe of his garment; for she said to herself, "If I only touch his garment, I shall be made well." Jesus turned, and seeing her, he said, "Take heart, daughter; your faith has made you well." And instantly the woman was made well. And when Jesus came to the ruler's house, and saw the flute players, and the crowd making a tumult, he said, "Depart; for the girl is not dead but sleeping." And they laughed at him. But when the crowd had been put outside, he went in and took her by the hand, and the girl arose. And the report of this went through all that district.

9:27-31

And as Jesus passed on from there, two blind men followed him, crying aloud. "Have mercy on us, Son of David." When he entered the house, the blind men came to him; and Jesus to them, "Do you believe that I am able to do this?" They said to him, "Yes, Lord." Then he touched their eyes, saying, "According to your faith be it done to you." And their eyes were opened. And Jesus sternly charged them, "See that no one knows it." But they went away and spread his fame through all that district.

9:32-33

As they were going away, behold, a dumb demoniac was brought to him. And when the demon had been cast out, the dumb man spoke; and the crowds marveled, saying, "Never was anything like this seen in Israel."

9:35

And Jesus went about all the cities and villages, teaching in their synagogues and preaching the gospel of the kingdom and healing every disease and every infirmity.

10:1

And he called to him his twelve disciples and gave them authority over unclean spirits, to cast them out, and to heal every disease and every infirmity.

12:9-13

And he went on from there and entered their synagogue. And behold, there was a man with a withered hand. And they asked him, "Is it lawful to heal on the sabbath?" so that they might accuse him. He said to them, "What man of you, if he has one sheep and it falls into a pit on the sabbath, will not lay hold of it and lift it out? Of how much more value is a man than a sheep! So it is lawful to do good on the sabbath." Then he said to the man, "Stretch out your hand." And the man stretched it out, and it was restored, whole like the other.

12:22

Then a blind and dumb demoniac was brought to him, and he healed him, so that the dumb man spoke and saw.

14:14

As he went ashore, he saw a great throng; and he had compassion on them, and he healed their sick.

14:34-36

And when they had crossed over, they came to land at Gennesaret. And when the men of that place recognized him, they sent round to all that region and brought to him all that were sick and besought him that they might only touch the fringe of his garment; and as many as touched it were made well.

15:21-28

And Jesus went away from there and withdrew to the district of Tyre and Sidon. And behold, a Canaanite woman from the region came out and cried, "Have mercy on me, O Lord. Son of David, my daughter is severely possessed by a demon." But he did not answer her a word. And his disciples came and begged him, saying, "Send her away, for she is crying after us." He answered, "I was sent only to the lost sheep of the house of Israel." But she came and knelt before him, saying, "Lord, help me." And he answered, "It is not fair to take the children's bread and throw it to the dogs." She said, "Yes, Lord, yet even the dogs eat the crumbs that fall from their master's table." Then Jesus answered her, 'O woman, great is your faith! Be it done for you as you desire." And her daughter was healed instantly.

15:29-31

And Jesus went on from there and passed along the Sea Galilee. And he went up the hills and sat down there. And great crowds came to him, bringing with them the lame, the maimed, the blind, the dumb, and many others, and they put them at his feet, and he healed them, so that the throng wondered, when they saw the dumb speaking, the maimed whole, the lame walking, and the blind seeing; and they glorified the God of Israel.

17:14-21

And when they came to the crowd, a man came up to him and kneeling before him said, "Lord, have mercy on my son, for he is an epileptic and suffers terribly; for often he falls into the fire, and often into the water. And I brought him to your disciples, and they could not heal him." And Jesus answered, "O faithless and perverse generation, how long am I to be with you? How long am I to bear with you? Bring him here to me." And Jesus rebuked him, and the demon came out of him, and the boy was cured instantly. Then the disciples came to Jesus privately and said, "Why could we not cast it out?" He said to them, "Because of your little faith. For truly, I say to you, if you have faith as a grain of mustard seed, you will say to this mountain, 'Move hence to yonder place.' and if will move; and nothing will be impossible to you."

19:1-2

Now when Jesus had finished these sayings, he went away from Galilee and entered the region of Judea beyond the Jordon; and large crowds followed him, and he healed them there.

20:29-34

And as they went out of Jericho, a great crowd followed him. And behold, two blind men sitting by the roadside, when they heard that Jesus was passing by, cried out, "Have mercy on us, Son of David!" The crowd rebuked them, telling them to be silent, but they cried out more,

"Lord, have mercy on us, Son of David!" And Jesus stopped and called them, saying, "What do you want me to do for you?" They said to him, "Lord, let our eyes be opened." And Jesus, in his pity, touched their eyes, and immediately they received their sight and followed him.

21:14

And the blind and the lame came to him in the temple, and he healed them.

Mark

1:21-27

And they went into Capernaum; and immediately on the sabbath he entered the synagogue and taught. And they were astonished at his teaching, for he taught them as one who had authority, and not as the scribes. And immediately there was in their synagogue a man with an unclean spirit; and he cried out, "What have you to do with us, Jesus of Nazareth? Have you come to destroy us? I know who you are, the Holy One of God." But Jesus rebuked him, saying, "Silent, and come out of him!" And the unclean spirit, convulsing him and crying with a loud voice, out of him. And they were all amazed, so that they questioned among themselves, saying, "What is this? A new teaching! With authority, he commands even the unclean spirits, and they obey him."

1:29-31

And immediately he left the synagogue; and entered the house of Simon and Andrew, with James and John. Now Simon's mother-in-law lay sick with a fever, and immediately they told him of her. And he came and took her by the hand and lifted her up, and the fever left her; and she served them.

1:32-34

That evening, at sundown, they brought to him all who were sick or possessed with demons. And the whole city was gathered together about the door. And he healed many who were sick with various diseases, and cast out many demons; and he would not permit the demons to speak, because they knew him.

1:40-45

And a leper came to him beseeching him, and kneeling said to him, "If you will, you can make me clean." Moved with pity, he stretched out his hand and touched him, and said to him, "I will; be clean." And immediately the leprosy left him, and he was made clean. And he sternly charged him, and sent him away at once, and said to him,

"See that you say nothing to anyone; but go, show yourself to the priest, and offer for your cleansing what Moses commanded, for proof to the people." But he went out and began to talk freely about it, and to spread the news, so that Jesus could no longer openly enter a town, but was out in the country; and people came to him from every quarter.

2:1-12

And when he returned to Capernaum after some days, it was reported that he was home. And many were gathered together, so that there was no longer room for them, not even about the door; and he was preaching the word to them. And they came, bringing to him a paralytic carried by four men. And when they could not get near him because of the crowd, they removed the roof above him; and they had made an opening, they let the pallet on which he paralytic lay. And when Jesus saw their faith, he said to the paralytic, "My son, your sins are forgiven." Now some of the scribes were sitting there, questioning in their hearts, "Why does this man speak thus? It is blasphemy! Who can forgive sin but God alone?" And immediately Jesus, perceiving in his spirit that they thus questioned within themselves, said to them, "Why do you question thus in your hearts? Which is easier, to say to the paralytic, 'Your sins are forgiven,' or to say, 'Rise, take up your pallet and walk'? But that you may know that the Son of man has authority on earth to forgive sins," he said to the paralytic, "I say to you, rise, take up your pallet and go home." And he rose, and immediately took the pallet and when out before them all; so that they were all amazed and glorified God, Saying, "We never saw anything like this!"

3:1-5

Again, he entered the synagogue, and a man was there who had a withered hand. And they watched him, to see whether he would heal him on the sabbath, so that they might accuse him. And he said to the man who had the withered hand, "Come here." And he said to them, "Is it lawful on the sabbath to do good or to do harm, to save life or to kill?" But they were silent. And he looked around at them with anger, grieved at their hardness of heart, and said to the man, "Stretch out your hand." He stretched it out, and his hand was restored.

3:9-11

And he told his disciples to have a boat ready for him because of the crowd, lest they should crush him; for he had healed many, so that all who had diseases pressed upon him to touch him. And whenever the unclean spirits beheld him, they fell down before him and cried out, "You are the Son of God."

6:4-6

And Jesus said to them, "A prophet is not without honor in his own country, and among his own kin, and in his own house." And he could do no mighty work there, except that he laid his hands upon a few sick people and healed them. And he marveled because of their unbelief.

6:53-56

And when they had crossed over, they came to land at Gennesaret, and moored to the shore. And when they got out of the boat, immediately the people recognized him, and ran about the whole neighborhood and began to bring sick people on their pallets to any place where they heard he was. And wherever he came, in villages, cities, or country, they laid the sick in the marketplaces, and besought him that they might touch even the fringe of his garment; and as many as touched it were made well.

7:31-36

Then he returned from the region of Tyre, and went through Sidon to the Sea of Galilee, through the region of the Decapolis. And they brought to him a man who was deaf and had an impediment in his speech; and they besought him to lay his hand upon him. And taking him aside from the multitude privately, he put his fingers into his ears, and he spat and touched his tongue; and looking up to heaven, he sighed, and said to him, "Ephphatha," that is, "Be opened." And his ears were opened, his tongue was released, and he spoke plainly. And he charged them to tell no one; but the more he charged them, the more zealously they proclaimed it.

8:22-26

And they came to Bethsaida. And some people brought to him a blind man and begged him to touch him. And he took the blind man by the hand, and led him out of the village; and when he had spit on his eyes and laid his hands upon him, he asked him, "Do you see anything?" And he looked up and said, "I see men, but they look like trees, walking." Then again, he laid his hands upon his eyes, and he looked intently and was restored, and saw everything clearly. And he sent him away to his home, saying, "Do not even enter the village."

9:17-29

And one of the crowd answered him, "Teacher, I brought my son to you, for he a dumb spirit; and wherever it seizes him, it dashes him down; and he foams and grinds his teeth and becomes rigid; and I asked your disciples to cast it out, they were not able. And he answered them, "O faithless generation, how long am I to be with you? How long am I to bear with you? Bring him to me." And they brought the boy to him; and when the spirit saw him, immediately it convulsed the boy, and he fell on the ground and rolled about, foaming at the mouth. And Jesus asked his father, "How long has had this?" And he said, "From childhood. And it has often cast him into the fire and into the water, to destroy him; but of you can do anything, have pity on us and help us." And Jesus said to him, "If you can! All things are possible to him who believes." Immediately, the father of the child cried out and said, "I believe; help my unbelief! And when Jesus saw that a crowd came running together, he rebuked the unclean spirit, saying to it, "You dumb and deaf spirit, I command you come out of him, and never enter him again." And after crying out and convulsing him terribly, it came out, and the boy was like a corpse; so that most of them said, "He is dead." But Jesus took him by the hand and lifted him up, and he arose. And when he had entered the house, his disciples asked him privately, "Why could we not cast it out?" And he said to them, "This kind cannot be driven out by anything but prayer."

10:46-52

And they came to Jericho; and as he was leaving Jericho with his disciples and a great multitude, Bartimaeus, a blind beggar, the son of Timaeus, was sitting by the roadside. And when he heard that it was Jesus of Nazareth, he began to cry out and say, "Jesus, Son of David, have mercy on me!" And many rebuked him, telling him to be silent; but he cried out all the more, "Son of David, have mercy on me!" And Jesus stopped and said, "Call him." And they called the blind man, saying to him, "Take heart; rise, he is calling you." And throwing off his mantle, he sprang up and came to Jesus. And Jesus said to him, "What do you want me to do for you?" And the blind man said to him, "Master, let me receive my sight." And Jesus said to him, "Go your way; your faith has made you well." And immediately he received his sight and followed him on the way.

Luke

4:38-39

And he arose and left the synagogue and entered Simon's house. Now, Simon's mother-in-law was ill with a high fever, and they besought him for her. And he stood over her and rebuked the fever, and it left her; and immediately she rose and served them.

4:40

Now, when the sun was setting, all those who had any that were sick with various diseases brought them to him; and he laid his hands on every one of them and healed them.

5:12-15

While he was in one of the cities, there came a man full of leprosy; and when he saw Jesus, he fell on his face and besought him, "Lord, if you will, you can make me clean." And he stretched out his hand, and touched him, saying, 'I will be clean." And immediately the leprosy left him. And he charged him to tell no one; but "go and show yourself to the priest, and make an offering for cleansing, as Moses commanded, for a proof to the people." But so much the more the report went abroad concerning him; and great multitudes gathered to hear and to be healed of their infirmities.

5:17-26

On one of those days, as he was teaching, there were Pharisees and teachers of the law sitting by, who had come from every village of Galilee and Judea and from Jerusalem; and the power of the Lord was with him to heal. And behold, men were bringing on a bed a man who was paralyzed, and they sought to bring him in and lay him before Jesus, but finding no way to bring him in, because of the crowd, they went on roof and let him down with his bed through the tiles into the midst before Jesus. And when he saw their faith, he said, "Man, your sins are forgiven you." And scribes and the Pharisees began to question, saying, "Who is this that speaks blasphemies? Who can forgive sins but God only?" When Jesus perceived their questionings, he answered them, "Why do you question in your hearts? Which is easier, to say, 'Your sins are forgiven you,' or to say, 'Rise and walk'? But that you may know that the Son of man has authority on earth to forgive sins," - he said to the man who was paralyzed- "I say to you, rise, take up your bed and go home." And immediately he rose before them, and took up that on which he lay, and went home, glorifying God. And amazement seized them all, and they glorified God and were filled with awe, saying, "We have seen strange things today."

6:6-10

On another sabbath, when he entered the synagogue and taught, a man was there whose right hand was withered. And the scribes and the Pharisees watched him, to see whether he would heal on the sabbath, so that they might find an accusation against him. But he knew their thoughts, and he said to the man who had the withered hand, "Come and stand here." And he rose and stood there. And Jesus said to them, "I ask you, is it lawful on the sabbath to do good or to do harm, to save life or to destroy it?" And he looked around on them all, and said to him, "Stretch out your hand." And he did so, and his hand was restored.

6:17-19

And he came down with them and stood on a level place, with a great crowd of his disciples and a great multitude of people from all Judea and Jerusalem and the seacoast of Tyer and Sidon, who came to hear him and be healed of their diseases; and those who were troubled with unclean spirits were cured. And all the crowd sought to touch him, for power came forth from him and healed them all.

7:1-10

After he had ended all his sayings in the hearing of the people, he entered Capernaum. Now, a centurion had a slave who was dear to him, who was sick and at the point of death. When he heard of Jesus, he sent to him elders of the Jews, asking him to come and heal his slave. And when they came to Jesus, they besought him earnestly, saying, "He is worthy to have you do this for him, for he loves our nation, and he built us our synagogue." And

Jesus went with them. When he was not far from the house, the centurion sent friends to him, saying to him, "Lord, do not trouble yourself, for I am not worthy to have you come under my roof; therefore I did not presume to come to you. But say the word, and let my servant be healed. For I am a man set under authority, with soldiers under me: and I say to one, 'Go.' And he goes; and to another, 'Come.' And he comes; and to my slave, 'Do this,' and he does it." When Jesus heard this, he marveled at him, and turned and said to the multitude that followed him, "I tell you not even in Israel have I found such faith." And when those who had been sent returned to the house, they found the slave well.

7:11-17

Soon afterward, he went to a city called Nain, and his disciples and a great crowd went with him. As he drew near to the gate of the city, behold, a man who had died was being carried out, the only son of his mother, and she was a widow; and a large crowd from the city was with her. And when the Lord saw her, he had compassion on her and said to her, "Do not weep." And he came and touched the bier, and the bearers stood still. And he said, "Young man, I say to you, arise." And the dead man sat up, up, and began to speak. And he gave him to his mother. Fear seized them all, and they glorified God, saying, "A great prophet has arisen among us!" and "God has visited his people!" And this report concerning him spread through the whole of Judea and all the surrounding country.

7;20-23

And when the men had come to him, they said, "John the Baptist has sent us to you, saying, 'Are you he who is to come, or shall we look for another?" In that hour, he cured many diseases and plagues and evil spirits, and on many that were blind he bestowed sight. And he answered them, "Go and tell John what you have seen and heard; the blind receive their sight, the lame walk, lepers are cleansed, and the deaf hear, the dead are raised up, the poor have good news preached to them. And blessed is he who takes no offence at me."

8:40-56

Now, when Jesus returned, the crowd welcomed him, for they were all waiting for him. And there came a man named Jairus, who was a ruler of the synagogue; and falling at Jesus' feet, he besought him to come to his house, for he had an only daughter, about twelve years of age, and she was dying.

As he went, the people pressed round him. And a woman who had had a flow of blood for twelve years and could not be healed by anyone, came up behind him, and touched the fringe of his garment; and immediately her flow of blood ceased. And Jesus said, "Who was it that touched me?" When all denied it, Peter said, "Master, the multitudes surround you and press upon you!" But Jesus said, "Someone touched me, for I perceive that power has gone forth from me." And when the woman saw that she was not hidden, she came trembling and falling down before him, declared in the presence of all the people why she had touched him, and how she had been immediately healed. And he said to her, "Daughter, your faith has made you well; go in peace."

While he was still speaking, a man from the ruler's house came and said, "Your daughter is dead; do not trouble the Teacher anymore." But Jesus, on hearing this, answered him, "Do not fear; only believe, and she shall be well." And when he came to the house, he permitted no one to enter with him, except Peter and John and James, and the father and mother of the child. And all were weeping and bewailing her; but he said, "Do not weep; for she is not dead but sleeping." And they laughed at him, knowing that she was dead. But taking her by the hand, he called, saying, "Child, arise." And her spirit returned, and she got up at once; and he directed that something should be given her to eat. And her parents were amazed, but he charged them to tell no one what had happened.

9:11

When the crowds learned it, they followed him; and he welcomed them and spoke to them of the kingdom of God and cured those who had need of healing.

9:37-43

On the next day, when they had come down from the mountain, a great crowd met him. And behold, a man from the crowd cried, "Teacher, I beg you to look upon my son, for he is my only child; and behold, a spirit seizes him, and he suddenly cries out; it convulses him till he foams, and shatters him, and will hardly leave him. And I begged your disciples to cast it out, but they could not." Jesus answered, "O faithless and perverse generation, how long am I to be with you and bear with you? Bring your son here." While he was coming, the demon tore him and convulsed him. But Jesus rebuked the unclean spirit, and healed the boy, and gave him back to his father. And all were astonished at the majesty of God.

13:10-13

Now he was teaching in one of the synagogues on the sabbath. And there was a woman who had a spirit of infirmity for eighteen years; she was bent over and could not fully straighten herself. And when Jesus saw her, he called her and said to her, "Woman, you are freed from your infirmity." And he laid his hands upon her, and immediately she was made straight, and she praised God.

14:1-6

One sabbath, when he went to dine at the house of a ruler who belonged to the Pharisees, they were watching him. And behold, there was a man before him who had dropsy. And Jesus spoke to the lawyers and Pharisees, saying, "Is it lawful to heal on the sabbath, or not?" But they were silent. Then he took him and healed him, and let him go. And he said to them, "Which of you, having an ass or an ox that has fallen into a well, will not immediately pull him out on the sabbath day?" And they could not reply to this.

14:13-14

But when you give a feast, invite the poor, the maimed, the lame, the blind. And you will be blessed, because they cannot repay you. You will be repaid at the resurrection of the just.

17:11-19

On the way to Jerusalem, he was passing along between Samaria and Galilee. And as he entered a village, he was met by ten lepers, who stood at a distance and lifted up their voices and said, "Jesus, Master, have mercy on us."

When he saw them, he said to them, "Go and show yourselves to the priest." And as they went, they were cleansed. Then one of them, when he saw that he was healed, turned back, praising God with a loud voice; and he fell on his face at Jesus' feet, giving him thanks. Now he was a Samaritan. Then said Jesus, "Were not ten cleansed? Where are the nine? Was no one found to return and give praise to God except this foreigner? And he said to him, "Rise and go your way; your faith has made you well."

18:35-43

As he drew near to Jericho, a blind man was sitting by the roadside begging; and a multitude going by, he inquired what this meant. They told him, "Jesus of Nazareth is passing by." And he cried, "Jesus, Son of David, have mercy on me!" And those who were in front rebuked him, telling him to be silent, but he cried out all the more, "Son of David, have mercy on me!" And Jesus stopped and commanded him to be brought to him, and when he came near, he asked him, "What do you want me to do for you?" He said, "Lord, let me receive my sight." And Jesus said to him, "Receive your sight; your faith has made you well." And immediately he received his sight and followed him, glorifying God; and all the people, when they saw it, gave praise to God.

22:50-52

And one of them struck the slave of high priest and cut off his right ear. But Jesus said, "No more of this!" and he touched his ear and healed him.

John

4:46-53

So, he came again to Canna in Galilee, where he had made the water wine. And at Capernaum, there was an official whose son was ill. When he heard that Jesus had come from Judea to Galilee, he went and begged him to come down and heal his son, for he was at the point of death. Jesus, therefore, said to him, "Unless you see signs and wonders, you will not believe." The official said to him, 'Sir, come down before my child dies." Jesus said to him, "Go; your son will live." The man believed the word that Jesus spoke to him and went his way. As he was going down, his servants met him and told him that his son was living. So he asked them the hour when he began to mend, and they said to him, "Yesterday at the seventh hour the fever left him." The father knew that was the hour when Jesus said to him, "Your son will live"; and he himself believed and all his household. This was now the second sign that Jesus did when he had come from Judea to Galilee.

5:2-9

Now, there is in Jerusalem by the sheep gate a pool, in Hebrew called Bethzatha, which has five porticoes. In these lay a multitude of invalids, blind, lame, paralyzed. One man was there, who had been ill for thirty-eight years. When Jesus saw him and knew he had been lying there a long time, he said to him, "Do you want to be healed?" The sick man answered him," Sir, I have no man to put me into the pool when the water is troubled, and while I am going another steps down before me." Jesus said to him, "Rise, take up your pallet, and walk." And at once the man was healed, and he took up his pallet and walked.

9:1-12

As he passed by, he saw a man blind from his birth. And his disciples asked him, "Rabbi, who sinned, this man or his parents, that he was born blind?" Jesus answered, "It was not this man sinned, or his parents, but that the works of God might be manifest in him. We must work the works of him who sent me, while it is day; night comes, when no one can work. As long as I am in the world, I am the light of the world." As he said this, he spat on the ground and made clay of the spittle and anointed the man's eyes with the clay, saying to him, "Go, wash in the pool of Siloam" (which means Sent). So, he went and washed and came back seeing. The neighbors and those who had seen him before as a beggar said, "Is not this the man who used to sit and beg?" Some said, "It is he"; others said, "No, but he is like him." He said I am the man." They said to him, "Then how were your eyes opened?" He answered, "The man called Jesus made clay and anointed my eyes and said to me, 'Go to Siloam and wash; so, I went and washed and received my sight." They said to him, "Where is he?" He said, "I do not know."

11:14-15 21-27 42-44

Then Jesus told them plainly, "Lazarus is dead; and for your sake I am glad I was not there, so that you may believe. But let us go to him."

Martha said to Jesus, "Lord, if you had been here, my brother would not have died. And even now I know that whatever you ask from God, God will give you." Jesus said to her, "Your brother will rise again." Martha said to him, "I know that he will rise again in the resurrection at the last day." Jesus said to her, "I am the resurrection and the life; he who believes in me, though he die, yet shall he live, and whoever lives and believes in me shall never die. Do you believe this?" She said to him, "Yes, Lord; I believe that you are the Christ, the Son of God, he who is coming into the world."

"Father, I thank thee that thou hast heard me. I knew that thou hearest me always, but I have said this on account of the people standing by, that they may believe that thou didst send me." When he had said this, he cried with a loud voice, "Lazarus, come out." The dead man came out, his hands and feet bound with bandages, and his face wrapped with a cloth. Jesus said to them, "Unbind him and let him go."

Acts

3:1-10

Now Peter and John were going up to the temple at the hour of prayer, the ninth hour. And a man lame from birth was being carried, whom they laid at that gate of the temple which was called Beautiful to ask alms of those who entered the temple. Seeing Peter and John about to go into the temple, he asked for alms. And Peter directed his gaze at him, with John, and said, "Look at us." And he fixed his attention upon them, expecting to receive something from them. But Peter said, "I have no silver and gold, but I give you what I have; in the names of Jesus Christ of Nazareth, walk." And he took him by the right hand and raised him up; and immediately his feet and ankles were made strong. And leaping up, he stood and walked and entered the temple with them, walking and leaping and praising God. And all the people saw him walking and praising God, and recognized him as the one who sat for alms at the Beautiful Gate of the temple; and they were filled with wonder and amazement at what had happened to him.

9:32-35

Now, as Peter went here and there among them all, he came down also to the saints that lived at Lydda. There, he found a man named Aeneas who had been bedridden for eight years and was paralyzed. And Peter said to him," Aeneas, Jesus Christ heals you; rise and make your bed." And immediately he rose. And all the residents of Lydda and Sharon saw him, and they turned to the Lord.

28:7-10

Now, in the neighborhood of that place were lands belonging to the chief man of the island, named Publius, who received us and entertained us hospitably for three days. It happened that the father of Publius lay sick with fever and dysentery; and Paul visited him and prayed, and putting his hands on him healed him. And when this had taken place, the rest of the people on the island who had diseases also came and were cured. They presented many gifts to us, and we sailed; they put on board whatever we needed.

Revelation

21:3-4

"Behold, the dwelling of God is with men. He will dwell with them, and they shall be his people, and God himself will be with them; he will wipe away every tear from their eyes, and death shall be no more, neither shall there be mourning nor crying nor pain any more, for the former things have passed away."

Final Verses

I read a new chapter of the Bible every day and finish with the following verses that help give a peaceful start to each new day of challenges.

The Provers

1:2-8

That men may know wisdom and instruction, understand words of insight, receive instruction in wise dealings, righteousness, justice, and equity; that prudence may be given to the simple, knowledge and discretion to the youth – the wise man also may hear and increase in learning, and the man of understanding acquire skill, to understand a proverb and a figure, the words of the wise and their riddles.

The fear of the Lord is the beginning of knowledge; fools despise wisdom and instruction.

Hear, my son, your father's instruction, and reject not your mother's teaching.

Psalms

23:1-6

The Lord is my shepherd, I shall not want; he makes me lie down in green pastures. He leads me beside still waters; he restores my soul. He leads me in paths of righteousness for his name's sake.

Even though I walk through the valley of the shadow of death, I fear no evil; for thy art with me; thy rod and thy staff, they comfort me.

Thou preparest a table before me in the presence of my enemies; thou anointest my head with oil, my cup overflows. Surely goodness and mercy shall follow me all the days of my life; and I shall dwell in the house of the Lord forever.

Matthew

6:8-15

For your Father knows what you need before you ask him.

Pray then like this;

Our Father who art in heaven,

Hallowed be thy name,

Thy kingdom come,

Thy will be done

On earth as it is in heaven.

Give us this day our daily bread;

And forgive us our debts,

As we also have forgiven our debtors;

And lead us not into temptation,

But deliver us from evil.

For if you forgive men their trespasses, your heavenly Father also will forgive you, but if you do not forgive men their trespasses, neither will your Father forgive your trespasses.

7:12

So, whatever you wish that men would do to you, do so to them; for this is the law and the prophets.

John

3:16-21

For God so loved the world that he gave his only Son, that whoever believes in him should not perish but have eternal life. For God sent the Son into the world, not to condemn the world, but that the world might be saved through him. He who believes in him is not condemned; he who does not believe is condemned already, because he has not believed in the name of the only Son of God. And this is the judgment, that the light has come into the world, and men loved darkness rather than light, because their deeds were evil. For everyone who does evil hates the light and does not come to the light lest his deeds should be exposed. But he who does what is true comes to the light, that it may be clearly seen that his deeds have been wrought in God.

Acts

3:4-10

'Look at us." And he fixed his attention upon them, expecting to receive something from them. But Peter said, "I have no silver and gold, but I give you what I have; in the name of Jesus Christ of Nazareth, walk." And he took him by the right hand and raised him up; and

immediately his feet and ankles were made strong. And leaping up, he stood and walked and entered the temple with them, walking and leaping and praising God. And all the people saw him walking and praising God, and recognized him as the one who sat for alms at the Beautiful Gate of the temple; and they were filled with wonder and amazement at what had happened to him.

First Corinthians

13:4-13

Love is patient and kind; love is not jealous or boastful; it is not arrogant or rude. Love does not insist on its own way; it is not irritable or resentful; it does not rejoice at wrong but rejoices in the right. Love bears all things, believes all things, hopes all things, endures all things. Love never ends; as for prophecy, it will pass away; as for tongues, they will cease; as for knowledge, it will pass away. For our knowledge is imperfect, and our prophecy is imperfect; but when the perfect comes, the imperfect will pass away. When I was a child, I spoke like child, I thought like a child, I reasoned like a child; when I became a man, I gave up childish ways. For now, we see in a mirror dimly, but then face to face. How I know in part; then I shall understand fully, even as I have been fully understood. So, faith, hope, love abide, these three; but the greatest of these is love.

16:13-14

Be watchful, stand firm in your faith, be courageous, be strong. Let all that you do be done in love.

James

1:2-4

Count it all joy, my brethren, when you meet various trials, for you know that the testing of your faith produces steadfastness. And let steadfastness have its full effect, that you may be perfect and complete, lacking in nothing.

1:19-20

Let every man be quick to hear, slow to speak, slow to anger, for the anger of man does not work the righteousness of God.

REFERENCES

Holy Bible
Revised Standard Version
Copyright 1952

The Jefferson Bible
The Life and Morals of Jesus of Nazareth
Edition 2012

The Wahls Protocol
Copyright 2014 by Dr. Terry Wahls LLC

The Turn
https;//www.jointheturn.org

ACKNOWLEDGMENTS

I would like to extend my heartfelt thanks to the following individuals, whose support, encouragement, and contributions have meant so much to me throughout this journey:

Sherrie Papcun

Barbara Reck

Noreen Hollo

Mercy McCloskey

Holly Ambrose

Sara Jackson

Your presence in my life—whether through guidance, friendship, or inspiration—has made a lasting impact. I am truly grateful.

www.ingramcontent.com/pod-product-compliance
Lightning Source LLC
LaVergne TN
LVHW021122080426
835513LV00011B/1206